D Major Scale Book

for cello

Three Octaves

by Cassia Harvey

CHP137

©2013 by C. Harvey Publications All Rights Reserved.

www.charveypublications.com - print books
www.learnstrings.com - PDF downloadable books
www.harveystringarrangements.com - chamber music

The D Major Scale Book

Cassia Harvey

3

4

5

6

7

8

9

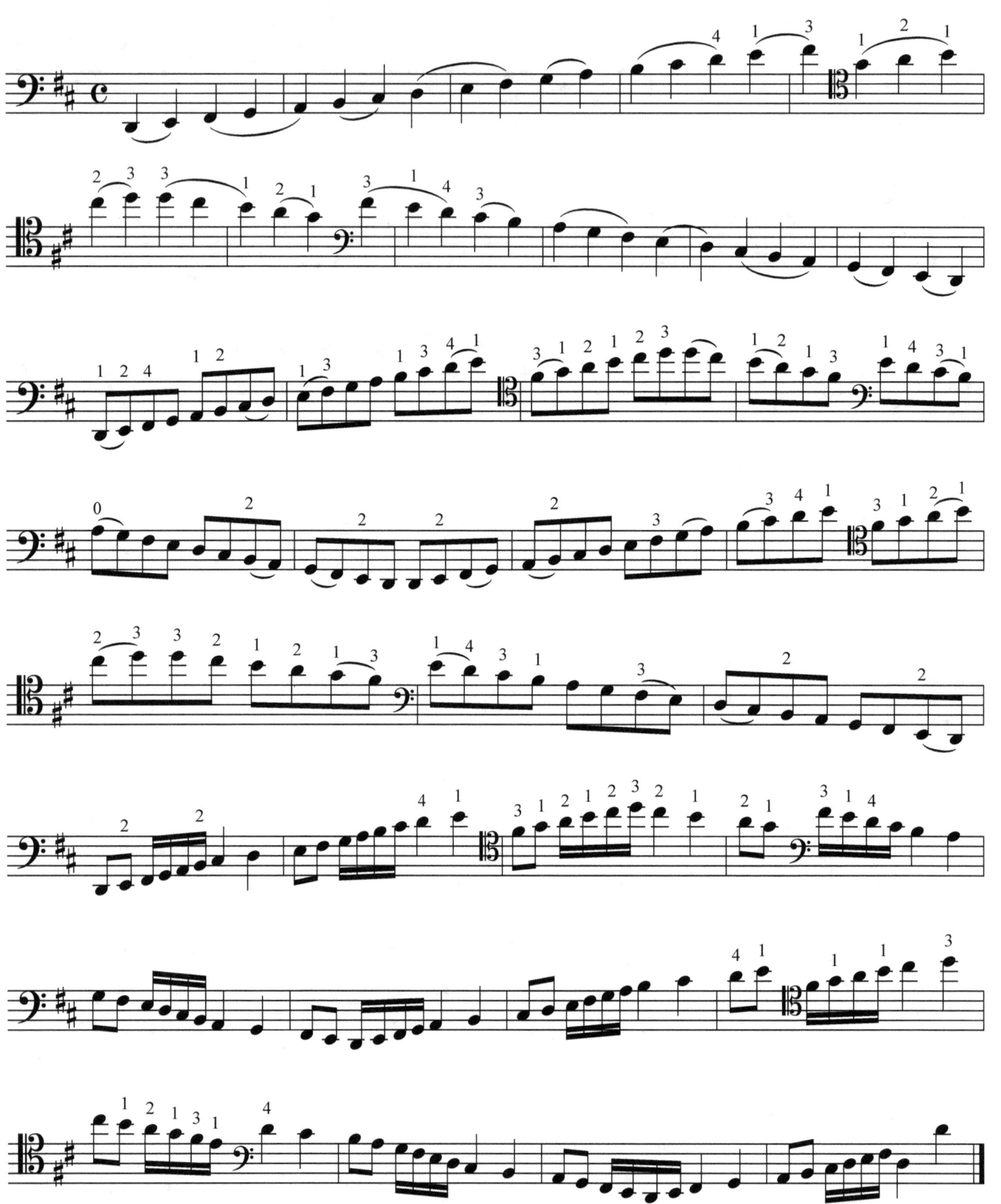

11

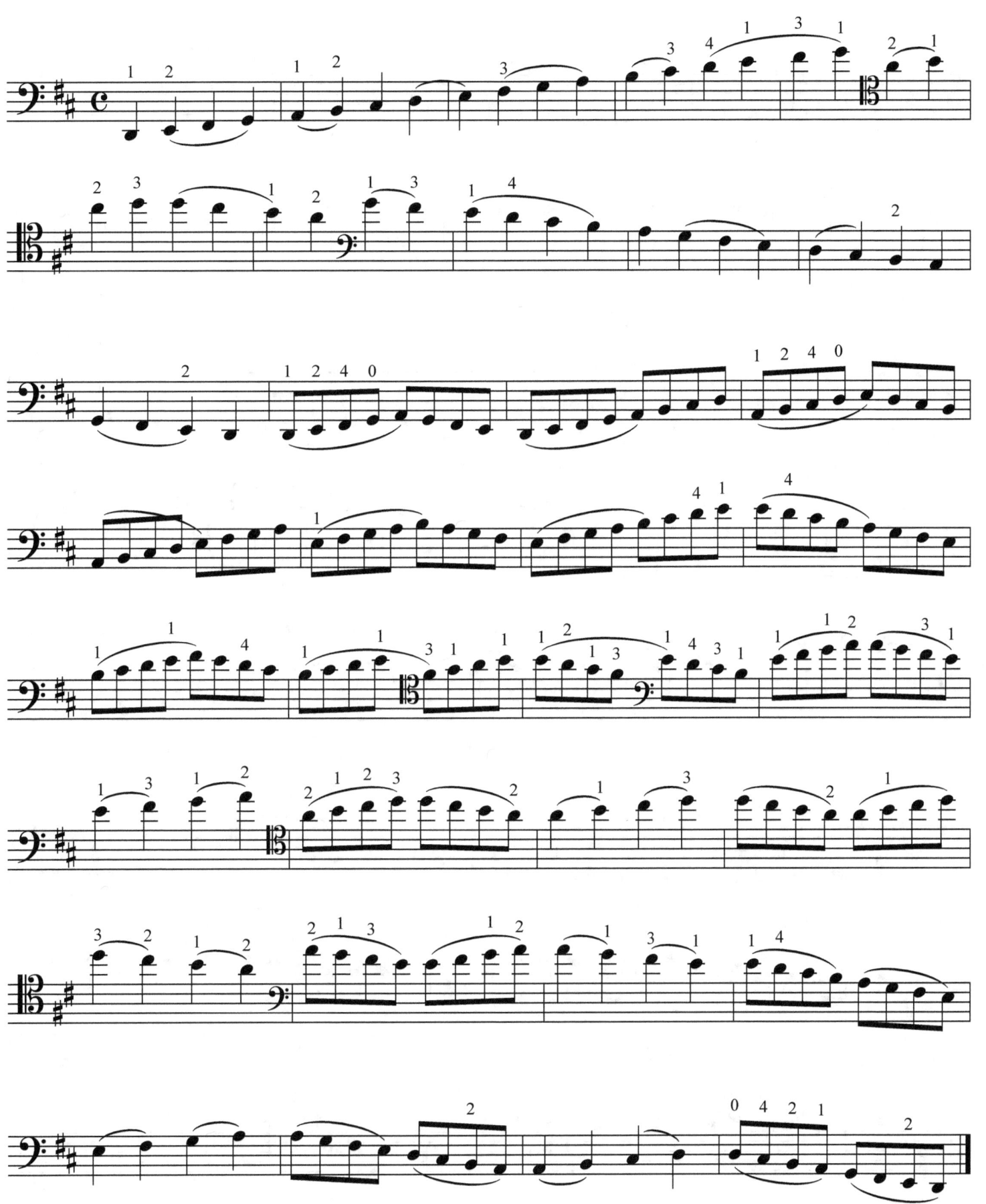

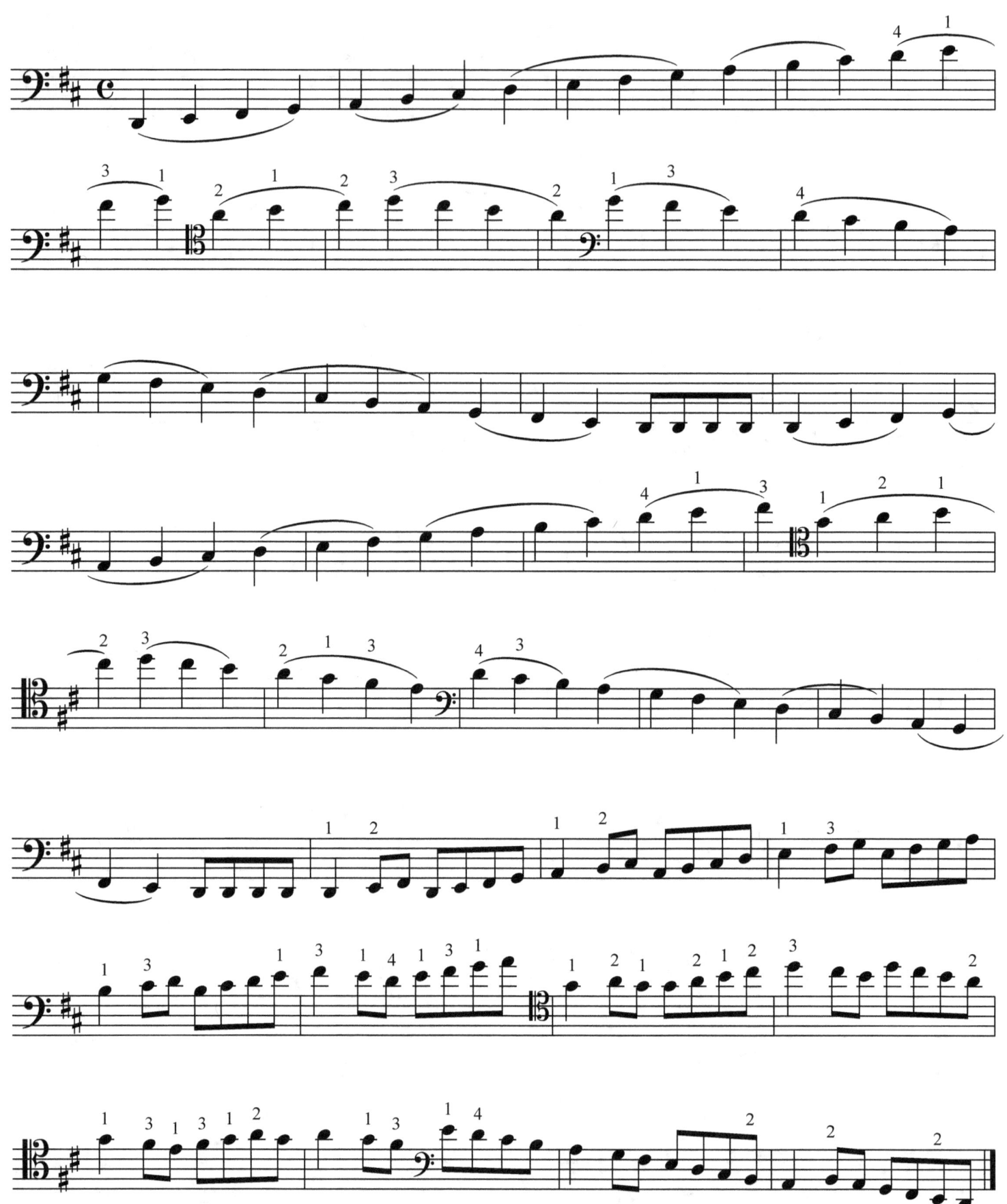

13

14

15

17

19

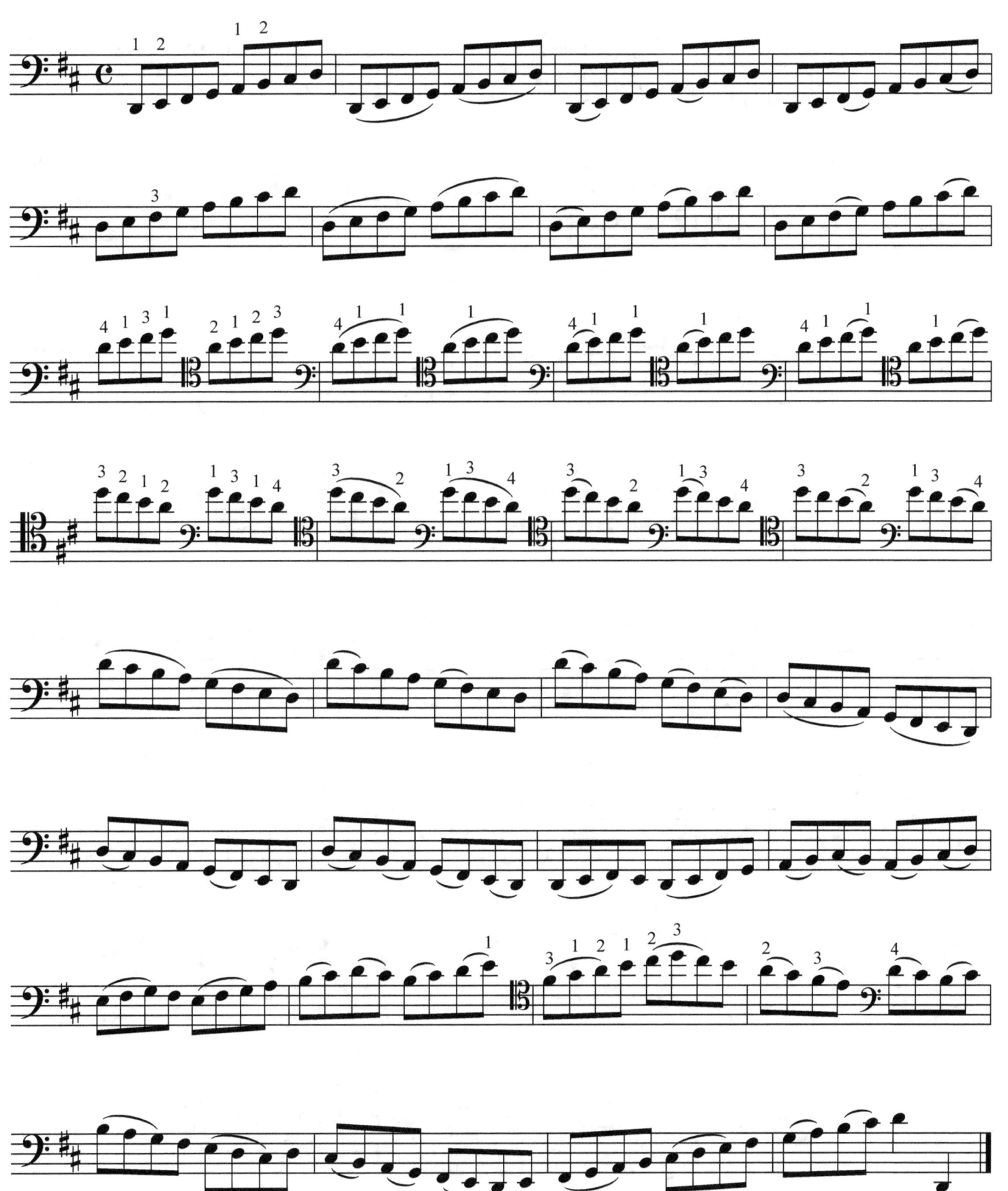

20

21

22

23

24

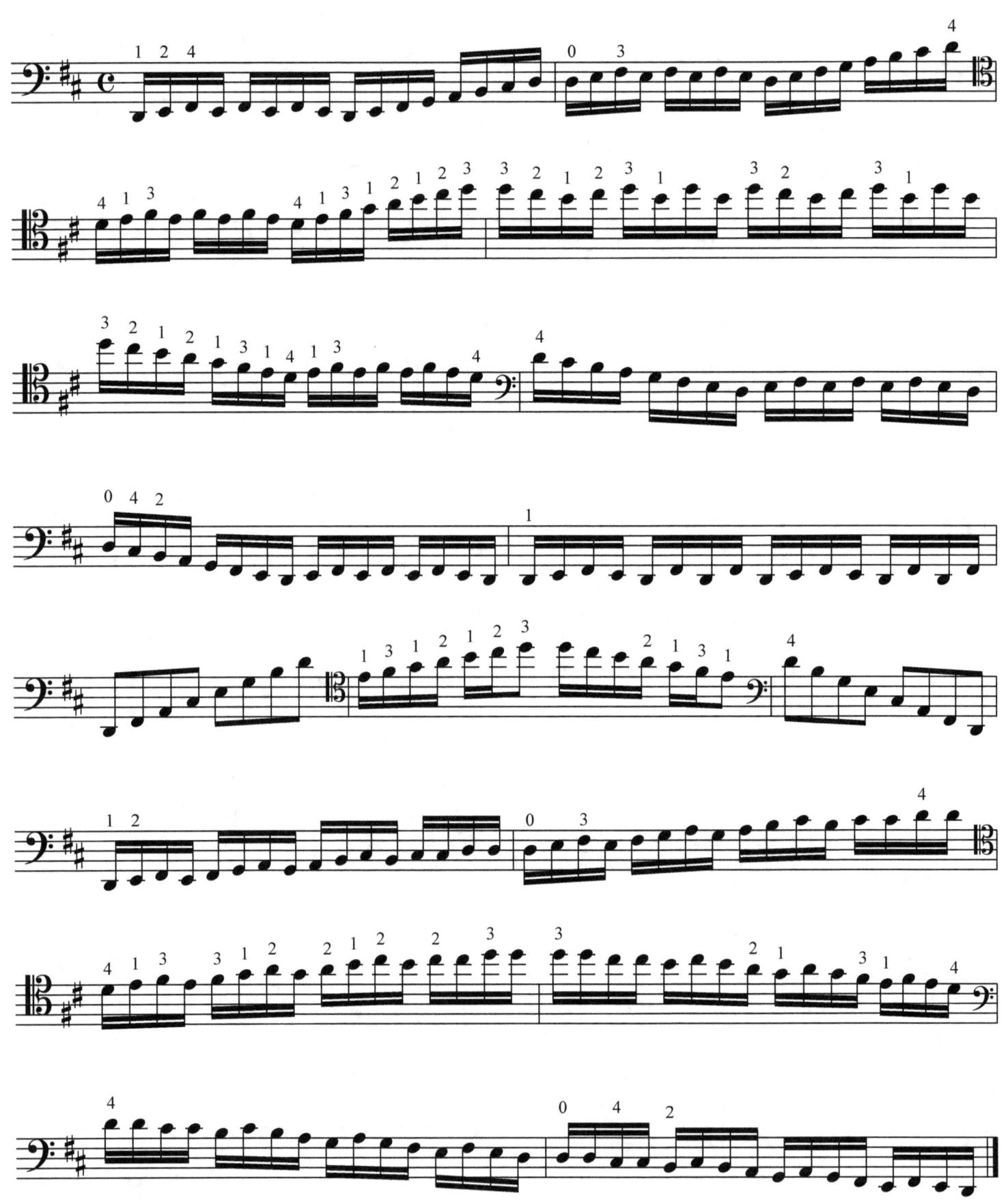

25

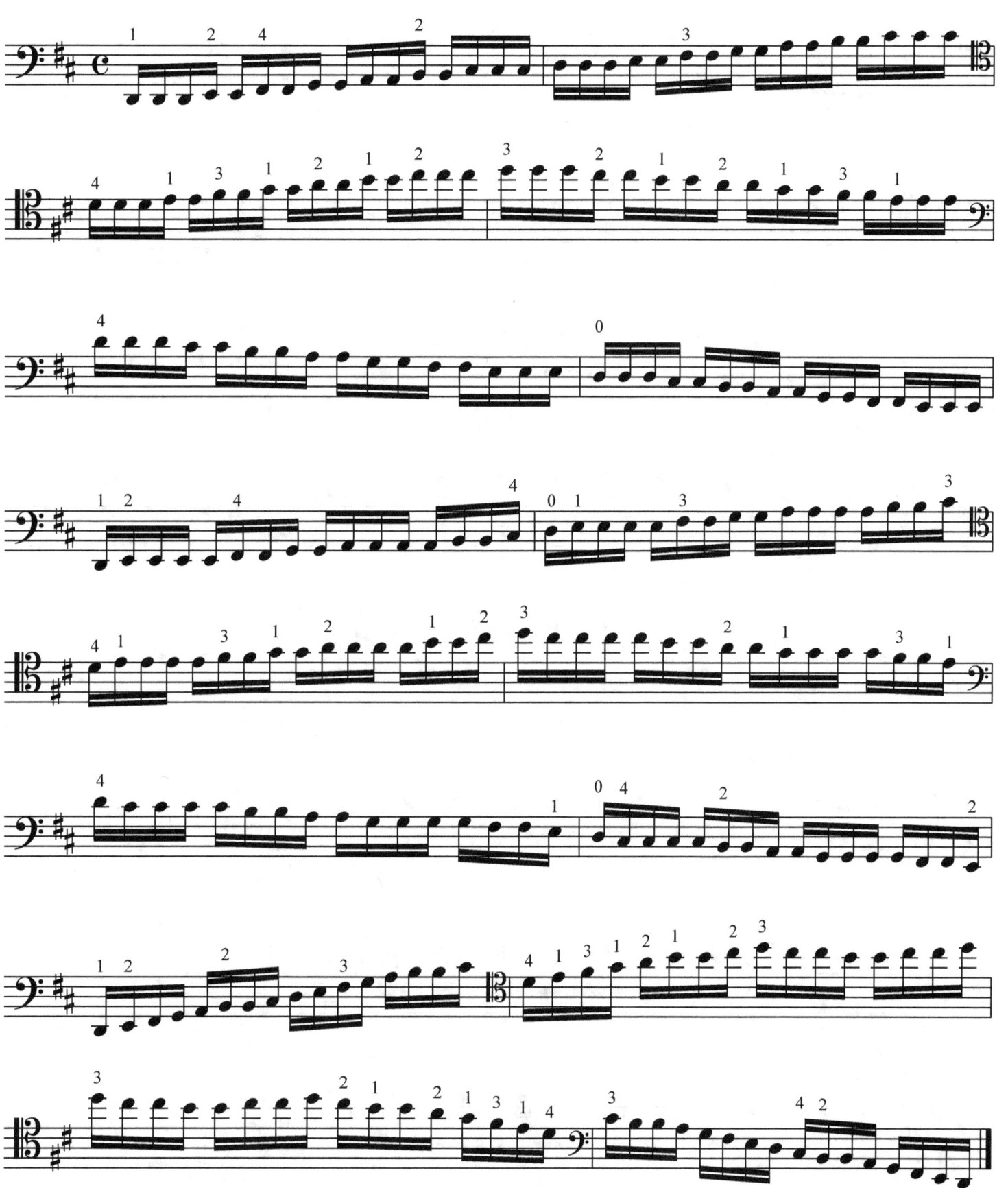

26

Also available from www.charveypublications.com: CHP356
Learning Three-Octave Scales on the Cello

Part One: Learning the Major Scales

C Major Scale

Cassia Harvey

©2019 C. Harvey Publications All Rights Reserved.